Martial Arts Masters

Chuck Norris

Dave Smeds

The Rosen Publishing Group, Inc.
New York

Published in 2002 by The Rosen Publishing Group, Inc.
29 East 21st Street, New York, NY 10010

Library of Congress Cataloging-in-Publication Data

Smeds, Dave.
Chuck Norris / by Dave Smeds. — 1st ed.
p. cm. — (Martial arts masters)
Includes bibliographical references (p.) and index.
ISBN 0-8239-3516-7 (lib. bdg.)
1. Norris, Chuck, 1940– 2. Martial artists—United States—Biography. 3. Actors—United States—Biography. I. Title. II. Series.
GV1113.N67 S64 2002
796.8'092—dc21

                                            2001002820

Manufactured in the United State of America

Table of Contents

Chuck Norris's on- and off-screen confidence came from standing up for himself and others while he was a teenager.

One day during his senior year of high school, Chuck Norris returned home to find his father in the living room. This should not have been. Chuck's mother, Wilma, had divorced Ray Norris more than a year earlier. Since then she had met, fallen in love with, and married George Knight. This was George and Wilma's house now, not Ray's.

Wilma was crying.

"What are you doing here?" Chuck asked his father.

"I'm waiting for George," he replied.

"Why?"

"I'm going to take care of him."

Ray's meaning was clear, and his breath smelled of alcohol, as usual. To Chuck, there was only one thing to do.

"No, you're not," the teenager stated. "You're not going to touch him."

Chuck and his father stepped outside to confront each other on the front lawn. Inside, Wilma rushed to the phone to call the police.

Chuck's father, a large, strong man, glared at his lightly built son. Chuck was afraid. He had always been afraid of his father. This time was different, however. This time

Chuck wasn't going to stand by and let his stepfather be attacked. He stood his ground.

In the end, Ray Norris could not bring himself to fight his own flesh and blood to get his way. He drove off in his car and never again had any meaningful involvement in the lives of his ex-wife and three boys, of whom Chuck was the eldest.

Chapter 1

Born to Hard Times

Young Chuck's brave act of standing up to his father matches the sort of heroism one would expect from Cordell Walker, the role Chuck Norris played on *Walker, Texas Ranger* for eight seasons. It is also typical of the tough, capable characters Norris played in a host of popular movies such as *A Force of One*, *Missing in Action*, and *Lone Wolf McQuade*. And, of course, it is what we would expect of a man who, before his acting career, won numerous karate championships, becoming one of the first superstars of the American martial arts scene.

In the late 1950s, though, few would have guessed Chuck Norris could ever amount to much. The day he faced off against his father was a turning point. On that day, in a symbolic way, he turned his back on his hard, poverty-stricken childhood and began to make himself into a world-class success, one step at a time.

A long, tall climb rose ahead of him, because Chuck Norris came from an extremely humble beginning. It is a mark of Chuck Norris's quality as a person that he does not complain about his early life. Rather than gripe about the insecurity of having a father who was seldom around, and who was often drunk when he was there, Norris prefers to speak of how well his mother turned any place they lived into a home. Thanks to Wilma and to other relatives, particularly Wilma's mother, Agnes Scarberry, Norris always had people he could depend on. He had roots.

Oklahoma Roots

Norris was born Carlos Ray Norris in Ryan, Oklahoma, on March 10, 1940. His first name was chosen in honor of Carlos Berry, the minister of the family's church in that small town at the southern border of the state, just across the Red River from Texas.

Rural Oklahoma is still a poor part of the United States, but in

Oklahoma farmers sit helplessly while their crops wilt in the fields from years of drought during the Depression.

1940 it was even worse. On top of the rigors of the Great Depression, its residents had endured the long years of the great drought known as the dust bowl. Many residents had already fled. Ray and Wilma Norris, an extremely young couple—Wilma was fifteen when they married—had chosen to stay near their families. Both Ray Norris and his bride were a mixture of Irish and Cherokee heritage, a blend common in Oklahoma.

With a new baby, however, Ray needed to find a good, steady job. The search for one, and the keeping of it, would take him away from home time and again. Sometimes Wilma and Chuck would join him, along with the family's second son, Wieland, born July 12, 1943. The family would move thirteen times in fifteen years.

During and just after World War II they spent short stretches in the San Francisco Bay Area while Ray worked in a naval shipyard. They tried Arizona for a year, in the hope that the dry air would help Wieland's asthma. They also lived in various places in Oklahoma, including the town of Cyril. But no sooner would they get settled than the Norris household would be uprooted again.

The problem was Ray Norris. He had come back from World War II with a bad leg and a drinking problem. Employers saw he was not dependable, and he failed to pin down jobs that allowed the family to stay put and thrive. Instead, Wilma often took herself and her boys to the safe haven of her mother's home. This was in the tiny community of Wilson, Oklahoma, about thirty miles east of

Ryan. To Chuck, Granny Scarberry's was "home," even though every period spent there was supposed to be temporary—"until things get better."

On the Move

By the end of 1949, Wilma, Chuck, and Wieland settled in southern California. But even then, they didn't stay in one spot. At first they lived in a trailer on a relative's land near Hawthorne, where Ray had found work at Bethlehem Steel. When Wilma became pregnant a third time, Ray disappeared, setting the family adrift again.

Unable to work and with Ray contributing little to the household income beyond his $30 monthly disability check, Wilma had to apply for welfare. When Aaron Norris was born in November 1951, Wilma and her boys had relocated to a shack in Gardena, California.

Wilma found a job as a silkscreen printer at Northrop Aircraft in late 1952. As a single parent with no money to pay a baby-sitter, she had no choice but to leave Chuck in charge of the house while she worked an evening shift. She came home from her first day of work to find Chuck outside in a rocking chair, holding Aaron. Rocking was the one thing that soothed the baby enough so that he would sleep.

Eventually Ray Norris showed up again, but his arrival only served to make a poor but happy household unpleasant. His drinking problem grew worse than ever. The only time it was under control was when he spent six months in a road camp serving a sentence for drunk driving, where he had no access to alcohol. When he became physically abusive, Wilma divorced him.

Better Times

Far from being a sad event, the divorce cleared the way for better times. Wilma met George Knight, a foreman at Northrop. With their marriage, Chuck finally had a positive male role model. George treated his stepsons with the love and firm guidance he showed toward his own three children. At seventeen, Chuck finally was able to emerge from the shell he had erected around himself. He no longer had to avoid making friends out of fear that those friends would see his run-down house and drunken father and

Norris's high school senior photo shows the looks of a future star. His family moved to Torrance, California in time for his high school graduation.

pity him. He didn't have to be ashamed of his situation.

The day that he stood up for his stepdad and sent his biological father on his way, Chuck knew that he was defending something important.

The making of Chuck Norris, the man, began that year, as he finished up high school in his family's new home community of Torrance, California. He would be the first to say that establishing a solid family unit of his own was the foundation of everything else he would do as an adult. Norris didn't waste any time. He asked Diane Holechek, a classmate of his at North Torrance High School, to go on a date. She accepted. Their romance blossomed. In December 1958, six months after his graduation, they became husband and wife.

Career Ambitions

Norris's concern, naturally, was not to make his father's mistakes. He

Like these high schoolers, Chuck Norris and Diane Holechek courted on the dance floor in the 1950s.

wanted the sort of solid, respectable career his father had never managed. Norris's choice was to be a policeman.

His ambitions were thwarted, however. The police academy didn't want him because he was so young and inexperienced. By making him postpone his plans, the powers-that-be did him a huge favor. If Norris had gone straight to being a cop, he would not be the star he is today.

As it was, Norris took a detour by enlisting in the air force. He knew that putting in time as a military policeman (M.P.) would greatly improve his chances of being accepted in a law enforcement job once he returned to civilian life.

Norris went through boot camp at Lackland Air Force Base. (His buddies there, thinking the name Carlos was too ethnic, began calling him Chuck. His family and old friends still call him Carlos.) Diane joined Chuck for a year after boot camp at his first posting at Gila Bend, Arizona. And then, in the midst of his hitch, destiny came calling.

Norris was assigned an isolated tour (meaning he couldn't bring family with him) at Osan Air Base in Korea. Stuck in a foreign country, forced to live a bachelor life, he needed something productive to do with his off-duty hours. Some of his buddies chose to spend their leisure time drinking. Norris, remembering that his father had acquired his drinking problem during his army days, refused to get caught up in that lifestyle. He turned instead to something that he felt would make him a better M.P. and candidate as a civilian police officer. He began studying martial arts.

Chapter 2

Finding His Calling

f Chuck Norris had been a larger man, he might never have become involved in martial arts. At five feet ten inches and weighing about 160 pounds, he was too small to control hefty men, a skill he needed in order to do his job. Back at Gila Bend he had once been called to remove a drunken sergeant from the non-commissioned officers (NCO) club. The sergeant, a mountain of a man, had thrown Norris across the room. And so when Norris

Norris learned judo to help him as a military policeman and to give him a hobby while stationed in Korea.

discovered that Osan Air Base had a judo club, he joined it.

Martial Arts Training

Back then, few Americans had seen the empty-hand fighting arts of Asia. Judo was the one Asian martial art Norris had heard of. Norris liked what he saw right away. Learning the skills was no easy task, however. He was only in average physical condition, and judo was quite different from the types of exercise he had done in the past. After two frustrating weeks, he broke his shoulder and had to take a break from training.

A few days after being injured, Norris was taking a walk and happened to see a class in tang soo do, a Korean martial art similar to karate. The style instantly appealed to Norris. His judo instructor agreed that Norris could switch to tang soo do while his shoulder healed, and gave him an introduction to the local tang soo do master, Jae Chul Shin.

Again, Norris was far from a natural at the art. He was not limber. He suffered through the stretching that began each class session. His feet grew swollen and sore from all the training on hard, bare ground. Nor did he receive helpful hints. The Korean approach to martial arts training was to let beginners keep up as best they could on their own. Norris tried to copy the moves of the people around him in the hope that eventually he would be good enough to be worthy of one-on-one feedback.

The ability Chuck Norris had that set him apart from most other beginners in the class was sheer determination. He worked out constantly, even though sessions lasted five hours. He trained six days a week, and took judo on Sundays. No matter how stiff and sore he was the next morning as he crawled out of bed to begin his M.P. duty shift, he stuck to his training schedule.

Norris had found something he could put his heart into. In high school, nearly all sports were team affairs. It was difficult to measure his success. If his football team did well, was it because of his contribution? In tang soo do, quality was measured on an individual basis.

Norris knew if he failed to kick high enough, spin gracefully enough, or breathe smoothly enough, he had only himself to blame. He was his own gauge. And so he trained and trained and trained.

Gradually, the Korean black belts in his group accepted him. Master Shin began to actively encourage him. After a year, the master announced that Norris was ready to test for black belt.

Shodan Tests

The test took place in Seoul, a long drive away over rough winter roads. Norris was the lone member of his school among 200 strangers, facing a panel of stern examiners, including Hwang Kee, the founder of tang soo do. The building was unheated, with the temperature below freezing. After four hours kneeling in place and going numb,

Norris forgot what he was supposed to do when his turn came. He failed.

Master Shin said nothing about Norris's failure. He simply continued to teach him. For three more months, Norris applied himself. Haunted by his failure, he came up with the psychological trick he would use again and again in his life as a tournament champion and as an actor. He rehearsed the test over and over in his mind, imagining himself doing everything right.

When Norris took the test a second time, he had no trouble. He was awarded his black belt. He came home from Korea as a *shodan,* a first-degree black belt, in tang soo do. He had also reached brown belt level in judo.

Back Home

When Norris first returned to the United States, his plan to become a policeman was still on track. Meanwhile, he settled in to finish the final phase of his four-year enlistment at March Air Force Base outside Riverside, California. Martial arts was still just a hobby. It was a hobby Norris loved, but not a way to make money or support a family.

Norris joined the judo club on base and soon was competing in air force judo tournaments. He enjoyed this, but was even more pleased when other soldiers saw him practicing kicks and asked him to teach them tang soo do. Their interest encouraged Norris to form a tang soo do club. It was an immediate success and quickly grew. Even the base commander, Lt. General Archie J. Old, joined the club. By the time Norris was discharged in August 1962, he knew that he had what it took to get lots of people interested in tang soo do.

A civilian again, Norris had one last obstacle to becoming a cop. There was a waiting list to get into the academy. Norris was facing a year or more just to get a chance to take the entrance examination. To get by in the meantime, he took a job as a file clerk at Northrop Aircraft.

The job didn't bring in much money. Feeling sure that he could attract paying tang soo do students, Norris began teaching classes in his father-in-law's backyard in Torrance to make ends meet. His brothers Wieland and Aaron became his first pupils.

His Own Dojo

Soon he had ten students and moved to a storefront dojo (a martial arts studio) in Torrance. By 1964, he had thirty students and had raised his rates.

That year he finally got his chance to apply to the police academy. He was prepared to quit his job at Northrop to do so. But he realized he no longer wanted to become a cop as much as he wanted to be a martial arts teacher. He did quit Northrop, but it was to open a second dojo in Redondo Beach and become a full-time instructor.

Within a year, he would be a champion as well.

Chapter 3

The Making of a Champion

Chuck Norris took a huge gamble by choosing to become a full-time martial arts instructor. The only way he could earn enough to support a family was if he attracted a lot of students. The Torrance and Redondo Beach dojos so far had enjoyed good luck pulling in local residents interested in something as new and different as martial arts. Also, Norris had such a likeable personality that a high percentage of those who tried his classes kept taking lessons. He had established a good base. But to really build up a large group of paying customers, Norris knew he had to make a name for himself.

A New Goal

There was one obvious way to build a reputation. By the 1960s the martial arts craze was riding high. Sport karate tournaments were cropping up all over the United States. They were not, however, limited to experts of actual karate styles such as shotokan or goju-ryu. Participants could be devotees of any Asian martial art that emphasized punching and kicking. Most important to Norris, the list included tang soo do.

Black Belt

VOL. I, NO. 1　　　THE MAGAZINE OF SELF-DEFENSE

● JUDO ● KARATE ● AIKIDO ● KENDO

SPECIAL JUDO ISSUE
Complete National AAU Finals

The popularity of martial arts in the 1960s sprouted magazines for enthusiasts such as *Black Belt*.

If he could win and become a tournament champion, Norris knew he would have no problem attracting students. This was no small goal. The quality of competitors had become quite high now that masters from Japan, Korea, and China had been in the United States long enough to develop top-flight students. Norris had no idea how well he might do. At twenty-four years old, he was already older than most contestants. He only knew that his financial health depended on his tournament success.

He had no luck at first. In the 1964 tournaments, he won a few preliminary rounds, but came home with no trophies. He made progress, and a few of his students won their beginner-level and intermediate-level competitions, but it wasn't enough to bring fame to his schools.

That only made Norris more determined. Meanwhile, Diane was expecting the couple's second child. Their first son Mike had been born in 1963 and was now a toddler. Norris had a full household to support. If things didn't improve, he knew he would have to get a different job and make martial arts a mere hobby again. At this point, he could barely afford the price of the gasoline needed to get to tournaments.

The Move

Norris came up with a plan. Since his early days in Korea, he had worked a lot on a spinning back kick. This move was performed by whipping his hips around and thrusting his leg out, catching his opponent with his heel. It was an unusual technique that few American sport karate competitors

The spinning back kick Norris perfected as a karate champion helped make his movie fights exciting.

had seen. Norris began to practice it over and over. Over many months, the kick became incredibly fast and powerful. It was not a kick defenders could easily stop or block. They could only hope not to be in the way when it came at them.

Norris's 1965 tournament season began with Tak Kubota's All-Stars Tournament in Los Angeles. Norris struggled through several bouts. Ultimately he reached the middle-weight finals, where he faced Ron Marchini, a powerful karate expert just entering his prime. A few years later Marchini would be named America's number one karate fighter by *Black Belt* magazine.

The bout came down to the final seconds. Norris and Marchini were tied, and Norris knew Marchini's clean, powerful performance throughout the day would cause the judges to award him the decision tiebreaker. Norris desperately needed to get in one last score. Marchini knew this, and was now playing defensively, waiting for the buzzer.

Norris charged in with a foot sweep, a punch to the ribs, and an open-hand strike to the neck. The corner judges' flags went up, giving Norris an ippon, a full point (a typical tournament score is only half a point). Norris had won. He came home with the middleweight championship trophy.

A victory at a regional event was only a start. Norris aimed higher with the California state championships. Again he claimed the middleweight championship. In addition, eleven of the twelve students he had brought with him won their matches. The Norris dojos were on the map.

Another Hurdle

Raising the stakes, Norris entered the Winter Nationals in San Jose, California. Norris again faced Ron Marchini. This time he went beyond the middleweight category and won the grand championship.

This win raised Norris to the top levels of competition. All he had left to win was a world-level event. Norris trained for the internationals, the most prestigious of all tournaments, to be held in August 1966 in Long Beach.

The internationals tournament was to be Norris's biggest challenge as a sport karate competitor. At the 1966 event he managed to take the middleweight division, but

Chuck Norris never stopped being a student of martial arts, studying new forms to help him win tournaments.

heavyweight fighter Allen Steen defeated him in the grand championship match.

Norris had gone as far as his secret weapon could take him. He was an excellent all-around fighter with solid skills, but now that he was in the spotlight, his opponents had the opportunity to study his moves. They began to see his spinning back kick coming. The cream-of-the-crop fighters figured out ways to deal with it.

Norris, however, had tasted success and liked it. Though he now had enough of a reputation to bring him more students, he wasn't ready to stop. He could be the best. How many times in life can someone be the best? After all his hard work, why should he settle for *almost* the best? He knew getting to the top wasn't a hopeless dream. He was in range. Only a quitter would stop.

Plain determination wasn't enough to get him past the last hurdle, though. The finest competitors then active—men like Allen Steen, Ron Marchini, Skipper Mullins, and Joe Lewis—were too good to beat simply by trying harder. Norris saw he needed to change two things about himself in order to defeat opponents of that caliber.

First, he needed to do the same thing to his competitors that they were doing to him. He needed to study them so that he could guess what moves they would use against him. After he had done that, he rehearsed his responses for months on end at his dojo, at his home, and finally off-stage at the tournaments themselves. He imagined exactly how his strategies would bring victory, never letting the image of himself as the winner fade from his mind. By the time he actually stepped into the ring, he burned with confidence.

Second, he had to become less predictable. The spinning back kick was his trademark and would always be one of his weapons, but he needed a broader menu of equally devastating attacks. To get them, he had to become a student again.

The Highest Mountain

Luckily, Norris's location in southern California kept him within reach of some of the finest martial artists he could ever hope to train with. He invited some of these individuals to his studios. He visited them at their dojos and homes. He compared techniques backstage at exhibitions and tournaments. He dedicated the year leading up to the 1967 internationals to cross-training with such masters as Fumio Demura of shito-ryu karate, Ed Parker of kenpo, Hidetaka Nishiyama of shotokan karate, and Gene LeBell, an expert in a wide range of combat arts from judo to wrestling to boxing. LeBell was of particular help because he could show Norris how to blend different styles to use against opponents.

Norris did not forget to prepare in one other essential way. He made sure to get in peak physical shape. To reach the finals of a grand championship meant fighting a dozen or more matches in a single day. If he was tired by the time he got to the finals, he would lose. Norris built stamina by working out constantly, and ate the right foods to give him energy.

In 1967, Norris competed in a string of tournaments, including:

- The North America Championships

- The All-American Championships

- The National Tournament of Champions

- The American Tang Soo Do Championships

- The Central Valley Championships

- The Tournament of Champions

- The All-American Open Karate Championships

Norris also competed in the International Karate Championships in Long Beach, the premier event of the year. He took the grand championship in each of the tournaments. It was an incredible performance. It would lead to him being named the Player of the Year by the Black Belt Hall of Fame and the Outstanding Fighter for the Decade of 1960–1969 by Who's Who in the Martial Arts, among many other honors. No one could have any doubt that Chuck Norris was the best karate tournament player on the circuit at the time, and one of the best of all time. He would never be forgotten.

Staying on Top

Norris repeated as grand champion at the 1968 internationals, as well as taking several other championships that year. He added two more championships in 1969, and shared in a U.S. team championship in 1970. He walked away from his career in 1974 holding the title of undefeated world middleweight karate champion. He had held the title for seven consecutive years.

During that span, he was also coaching and leading his students toward their own successes. From 1967 to 1969, Chuck Norris's Black Belt Karate Team went undefeated in eighty straight matches.

Norris was involved with organized sport karate until 1974, serving as a referee, judge, organizer, teacher, and sponsor. His incredible winning record assured that he would never lack students. By the time he withdrew from the scene he had founded thirty-two schools and nurtured hundreds of pupils to black belt level.

Norris's remarkable martial arts career gave him tremendous satisfaction. But he was not content to simply drift through the second half of his life. He set a new goal. He decided to become an actor.

Martial Arts Chuck Norris Has Studied

Martial arts are systems of movement based on combat forms. Many of these systems can be very effective in fighting situations. Some students learn them primarily to learn to defend themselves. However, they are considered "arts" because they are also designed to be studied for their own sake, as a type of personal expression. In other words, a student need not be interested in the fighting aspect. Instead, the student can devote himself or herself to practicing the moves because he or she finds them beautiful, or knows they are good exercise, or because they preserve the style of movement used by a revered teacher.

There are many kinds of martial arts from all parts of the world. In the past forty years, martial arts from the Far East, especially those based on unarmed combat, have become so popular that when an American hears the words "martial arts," he or she usually thinks of karate or some other Asian art, and not of a European combat form like fencing.

Chuck Norris was one of the pioneer instructors that helped make Asian martial arts well known in the United States. Over the years he has studied and taught a long list of them, including the following major types.

Jujitsu

Modern jujitsu is based on ancient Japanese hand-to-hand combat. The older form was very practical and very deadly, used by samurai, the Japanese warrior caste, in actual battle situations. In the late 1800s, after the samurai class had become less dominant, jujitsu was changed so that it could be practiced safely as an art form. Masters restricted their teaching to limited sets of moves. Today there are many types of jujitsu, but all involve close fighting such as grappling, throwing, sweeping, chokes, and holds. Chuck Norris learned choke moves from Al Thomas.

Judo

In the 1880s in Japan, a student of jujitsu named Jigoro Kano modified the art he had been taught so much that he gave it a different name. Judo means "gentle way." The moves Kano chose were those he felt could be performed safely and with rules suitable to sport competition. The heart of judo is its throws and foot sweeps (and learning how to fall properly). His creation became wildly popular and today is one of the most recognized and well-organized Asian martial arts of all, with millions of practitioners in Japan and hundreds of thousands elsewhere. It was recognized as an Olympic Games sport in 1964. Judo was the very first martial art Chuck Norris studied, and the first in which he competed. He later

Judo became an Olympic sport in 1964.

trained with Gene LeBell, who has taught many Hollywood stuntpeople.

Karate

"Karate" is a Japanese word for the empty-hand fighting arts that came from the island of Okinawa. Some Americans, such as Chuck Norris, also use "karate" to refer to Korean arts like tang soo do or Chinese arts like chu'an fa, because all these systems depend on punching, kicking, and blocking. There are many types of karate on Okinawa, but the four that attracted large numbers of students on mainland Japan during the twentieth century are shotokan, goju-ryu, shito-ryu, and wado-ryu. Chuck Norris looked to southern California shotokan instructors Hidetaka

The empty-hand fighting style of karate uses kicks, punches, and blocks to battle an opponent.

Nishiyama and Tsutomu Ohshima, and to shito-ryu teacher Fumio Demura, to polish his skills during his tournament years.

Tang Soo Do

This is Chuck Norris's main style, the first in which he became an expert. Norris's original tang soo do instructor was Jae Chul Shin. Korean in origin, tang soo do was developed in the mid-twentieth century by Hwang Kee. Like karate, its primary techniques are punching and kicking. Hwang Kee based his system partly on Chinese arts, but most of all on the ancient Korean art of soo bahk do, from which it gets its famous kicks, which are often aimed high on the opponent's body. In recent years, many tang soo do schools have become part of the World Tae Kwon Do Federation, the organization that makes the rules for Korean martial arts in the Olympic Games.

In the mid-1990s, Norris was awarded an eighth-degree black belt in tae kwon do, the highest rank ever earned by an American student.

Aikido

Aikido is a Japanese art form developed in the mid-twentieth century by Morihei Ueshiba. It concentrates on the grabbing of an attacker's wrists and elbows in order to throw the attacker down and immobilize him or her. As much time is spent learning to fall and roll properly as is studying the throwing/holding techniques. Chuck Norris was introduced to aikido by Jun Chung.

Kenpo

Kenpo is a branch of jujitsu made famous in America by Ed Parker, one of the first prominent U.S. teachers of Asian martial arts. (Kenpo is not to be confused with *kempo*, a Japanese word used to refer to chu'an fa, a branch of Chinese kung fu.) Chuck Norris learned kenpo directly from Parker.

Kung Fu

"Kung fu" is a term used in the United States to refer to the karate-like martial arts of China. In China, the term simply means "ability" or "skill." A better translation of "martial arts"is *wu shu*. There are hundreds of types of these Chinese forms, many quite different from each other. Some, like t'ai chi chu'an, are designed not as fighting arts, but as means to promote health and calm the mind. Chuck Norris picked up techniques from Bruce Lee that

Kung fu is a Chinese martial art form that has hundreds of different style varieties.

came from a southern Chinese style called wing chun, which Lee studied in Hong Kong under famous master Yip Man.

Chapter 4

Becoming a Star

Chuck Norris's first movie-making opportunities came thanks to his buddy, Bruce Lee, who was to go on to become the legendary star of *Enter the Dragon* (1973).

Chuck Norris and Bruce Lee first met at the All-American Championships at Madison Square Garden in New York in 1967. Lee, a struggling actor at that time but known to martial art fans for such roles as

Kato in the prime-time television show *The Green Hornet,* approached Norris to congratulate him. Norris had just defeated heavyweight Joe Lewis for the grand championship.

The two men hit it off at once. They couldn't stop talking. Since they were both staying at the same hotel, they rode back from the arena together so that they didn't have to end their conversation. Norris was bruised and battered from the day's matches, which had begun early that morning, but he couldn't resist lingering in the hallway leading to Lee's room. They stayed there until seven in the morning, exchanging techniques and comparing their martial arts philosophies. They left New York as firm friends.

Bruce Lee was a struggling actor when he met Chuck Norris in 1967. He later became a star.

Tips and Rolls

Lee was then living in Culver City, California. He and Norris would regularly get together in Lee's backyard for intense workouts, often followed by trips to Lee's favorite Chinese restaurant. Lee showed Norris techniques taken from wing chun, the Chinese martial art he had studied in Hong Kong. In return, Norris showed Lee how to master high kicks, which were not common in wing chun.

Lee was developing an approach to life and martial arts he called *jeet kune do*, "the way of the intercepting fist." According to its principles, a person should keep himself or herself ready for anything, and accept nothing less than the best from himself or herself. To Lee, that meant becoming the first actor of Chinese descent to be a major American film star. So far his biggest roles had been limited to television sidekick characters.

During most of their six-year friendship, which ended with Lee's untimely death in 1973 from an allergic reaction to a headache remedy, Norris was happy enough to experience the Hollywood world second-hand. An early exception came in 1968. Lee was serving as the stunt coordinator for the movie *The Wrecking Crew,* starring Dean Martin, Elke Sommer, and Sharon Tate. He used his influence to award a one-line role as a bodyguard to Norris.

Norris enjoyed seeing how films were made, but he hated how nervous he became when the camera turned toward him and how awkward his performance looked on the screen later. He decided he would stay away from acting in the future. He limited himself to appearing as himself, as when he did a commercial for Black Belt cologne and a walk-on role in the prime-time television comedy, *Room 222*. He avoided having to learn a character and speak lines from a script.

A Taste of Hollywood

Norris was, however, being increasingly drawn into Hollywood society. Thanks to his fame as a champion and the southern California locale of most of his schools, Norris was teaching martial arts to a growing list of film and television celebrities. These came to include such well-known people as Dan Blocker and

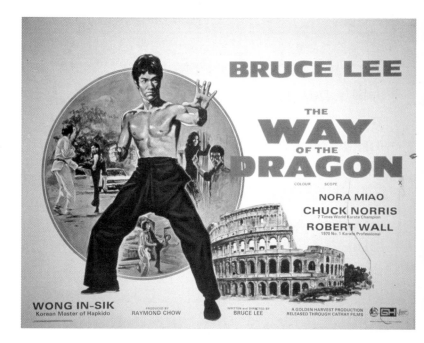

Chuck Norris appeared in one of Bruce Lee's martial arts movies in 1972.

Michael Landon of *Bonanza*, Bob Barker of *Truth or Consequences*, Priscilla Presley, Donnie and Marie Osmond, and Steve McQueen.

Finally, in 1972, Bruce Lee tempted Norris with a role he couldn't refuse. Lee was becoming famous as a star of martial arts films made in Hong Kong. He asked Norris to play his adversary in a key fight scene set in the Roman Coliseum for *Return of the Dragon*. Norris accepted.

Norris and his business partner Bob Wall, who was also in the movie, flew to Rome to film the big climax, and then on to Hong Kong to add a few supporting scenes. Lee got Norris through the nervousness, and Norris came home knowing he made a positive contribution to the project.

Return of the Dragon cost less than $250,000 to make. It eventually earned over $80 million. The fight scene between Norris and Lee became a classic.

Norris learned that he could, under the right conditions, work

The fight scene between Norris and Bruce Lee in *Return of the Dragon* is a classic of martial arts movies.

well in front of a camera and turn in a performance that audiences would adore. Not long after, his friend and student Steve McQueen, one of Hollywood's biggest stars of the era for movies like *Bullitt* and *The Great Escape,* suggested he try acting as a profession. Norris began seriously considering it.

A New Role

The fact was, as Norris withdrew from the tournament scene, pulling out completely in 1974, his life needed a new direction. He also needed money. In 1973 he took back the chain of martial arts schools that he and Bob Wall had sold in 1970. The various investors who had owned the schools in those three years had not operated them well. Large debts had built up. Norris didn't want his name associated with failed schools. He worked out plans to pay off the debts over time. The plan eventually succeeded, but during the mid-1970s Norris and Dianne were, in a sense, poorer than they had been in the early days of their marriage. He thought of how Bruce Lee had conquered Hollywood. With that as inspiration, he decided to take McQueen's advice.

Progress was slow. Norris managed to get a few small acting jobs, the best being a starring role in the minor film *Breaker! Breaker!* But he spent most of the next three years knocking on the doors of studios and production companies, trying and failing to get the kind of role that would ensure a real career. Among other things, he tried to convince producers and film investors to finance a movie called *Good Guys Wear Black*. The script was based on an idea by John Robertson, one of Norris's first black belt students, and written by one of Norris's screenwriter friends, Joe Fraley.

Finally Norris met Allen Bodoh of American Cinema, a small company with a couple of recent minor hits. Bodoh wondered why anyone would come to see Chuck Norris, an unknown, in a movie.

Norris explained that in the world of martial arts, he was not an unknown. The United States contained four million martial arts students. They all knew his name. If half of them came to see the movie a single time in the theaters at three dollars each, the movie would earn six million dollars. It would only take one million to make the film.

Bodoh saw the logic. Norris knew his audience. They were people like the kid he had been when he spent hours in the theater in Wilson, Oklahoma, watching heroic adventure pictures starring John Wayne or Gary Cooper—tales of good guys versus bad guys, and no mistaking which was which.

Good Business

Bodoh and his partner Michael Leone agreed to finance and produce *Good Guys Wear Black*, with Norris in the lead role. They made it and had it ready in 1977. The film did not have an easy time finding a distributor. When it finally did, it was released a few theaters at a time,

Chuck Norris worked tirelessly to get his first starring role in 1977's *Good Guys Wear Black*.

with almost no promotion. What little push it received came from the interviews Norris gave and the talk-show appearances Norris made as he toured the country in its support. The public did not become aware of it overnight.

Fortunately, Bodoh and Leone felt things had gone just well enough to try again. They hired Norris to do *A Force of One* (1979). It was only after *A Force of One* was already out that it became clear just how well these low-budget projects were doing. In its slow but steady initial run, *Good Guys Wear Black* earned $18 million. *A Force of One* earned $20 million. In the end, Norris's films for American Cinema, which also included *The Octagon* (1980), earned the company over $100

Though critics found Norris's acting ability shaky, his fans loved his movies' action and the good-versus-evil plots.

million, more than ten times what they had cost to make.

Critics ridiculed Norris's acting abilities, but the audiences loved the kinds of films he made. He had been right. Lots of people still wanted the sort of heroic adventures he had grown up with.

After *The Octagon,* Norris never had to worry about being poor again. He and Dianne were able to move into a big house. They knew they would be able to send Mike and Eric to any college they wished to go to. Norris had come a long way from his penniless, dust bowl beginnings.

Unlike others who have succeeded beyond their wildest imaginings, Norris did not lose sight of the important things in life. His sons were teenagers and needed a father in their lives. He made

Chuck Norris in *A Force of One*

time for them, even skipping a year of filming so that he could be home for Eric's final year of high school. And now that he was a bankable star with the authority to shape the kind of projects he worked on, he went for those that did more than make money or provide cheap thrills. Chuck Norris knew that fame should be used for a purpose. He was to become not just a star, but a role model.

Chapter 5

Living by
His Principles

In the mid-1970s, while studying acting under Estelle Harmon, another student in the class told Norris he simply didn't have what it took to be an actor. Yet within five years, Norris went from a struggling acting student to a major box office star, just as he had earlier gone from a know-nothing tang soo do student to an international champion in little more than seven years.

Norris reached both goals by applying the same approach. He would decide what he needed to do, then imagine himself doing it correctly over and over. In the beginning of his film career, he found it a challenge just to keep his lines memorized. So he rehearsed. He concentrated. He didn't let himself dwell on the ways he might go wrong.

Chuck Norris thrives on meeting challenges. That being the case, he has not stopped setting new goals for himself over the past twenty years.

Branching Out

After the success of the three American Cinema productions, it was no longer enough for Norris to just say his lines and hold down a steady job in films. He wanted to

Chuck Norris studied the finer points of acting in order to be more than just an action hero.

test his limits. The studio executives thought he belonged only in martial arts pictures. Norris wanted to do more acting than simply delivering a few lines of dialogue between fight scenes. He didn't want to be treated as little more than a stuntman.

Changing that impression of himself took time. In his early 1980s films, *An Eye for an Eye, Silent Rage,*

By the time Norris starred in *Silent Rage*, he was known in the film business as a professional who could be counted on to work hard.

and *Forced Vengeance,* Norris played characters that were cast in the same mold as his early roles. Those movies were attacked by the critics, but they were important to Norris for at least three reasons. One, they earned him enough money to afford to wait for better offers in the future. Two, they helped him work with different people, which not only gave him more experience, but showed those colleagues that he knew what he was doing. And three, he gained credit for the things he could control, the main thing being the quality of the fight scenes. Norris was given more authority to plan and guide the stunts, often with the assistance of his brother Aaron. He made sure to give the audience good value.

With Norris's movies consistently making money, the studios at last let

Norris's role as Lone Wolf McQuade helped him break the martial arts mold in which he had been typecast throughout the 1970s.

him make more of the story decisions. They agreed to make a movie called *Lone Wolf McQuade*, based on some of Norris's ideas.

Practice Pays Off

Norris's portrayal of James McQuade in the 1983 film was his breakout

Missing in Action was the first of three Vietnam war–based movies that Norris made in honor of his brother, Wieland, who had died in the war.

role. He didn't just fight. It wasn't just a "chop-socky flick" in the tradition of cheap Hong Kong movies. It was a full-fledged action-adventure film. Critics began to admit that Chuck Norris was a more talented actor than they had given him credit for.

Norris continued to have a major hand in the story lines of many of his pictures from then on. Most especially, he dedicated a trio of films to his brother, Wieland, who had died in Vietnam in 1970. These consisted of *Missing in Action* and its sequels, in which Norris played Colonel James Braddock. They remain among Norris's favorite films of his career because they are tributes to Wieland and because Norris feels he did some of his best acting in his prisoner-of-war scenes.

Norris's film career continued to flourish through the mid-1990s. His string of major motion pictures includes *Delta Force, Firewalker, Sidekicks, Top Dog,* and others. As this part of his career wound down, Norris shifted into an even bigger success, this time on television. Norris's long-running television series, *Walker, Texas Ranger*, has been his main occupation in recent years. Norris, with the help of his brother Aaron and a few close associates, served as the guiding force behind the show, which ran in prime time on CBS from 1993–2001 and in daily syndicated reruns on USA Network.

Reviewers were certain *Walker,* with its no-frills stories of right versus wrong, would fail in half a season. Instead, the show remained consistently near the top of the

Chuck Norris strikes a karate pose as he prepares to cut a cake marking the 100th episode of *Walker, Texas Ranger.*

ratings charts for eight years. It might very well still be in production had Norris not voluntarily chosen to "leave while on top" as he had done with his tournament career.

Career Success

What the critics failed to realize is how audiences respond to Chuck Norris. Fans can tell that Norris believes in the ideals that Cordell Walker, Texas Ranger stands for. Anyone can see how Chuck Norris has lived his life. In the past two decades, Norris has demonstrated the strength of his morals and the depth of his principles. For example, he has:

- Become a real police officer. This was not the same as the career he had aimed for in his youth, but

Norris finally became a real-life police officer while working on his hit TV show, *Walker, Texas Ranger.*

Norris served as a commissioned officer in Terrell, Texas. In 1996 and 1997 he helped in the arrests of over a hundred drug suspects.

🌓 Contributed his time and money to a host of charities, including Funds for Kids, the United Way, and the Veterans Administration National Salute to Hospitalized

Veterans. For many years he has visited sick children as part of the Make-A-Wish Foundation. In 1990, with President George H. Bush, he founded the Kick Drugs Out of America Foundation. This charity provides funds to teach kids in disadvantaged schools discipline through martial arts. The foundation has helped dozens of schools and thousands of kids.

Written books, delivered lectures, and given interviews highlighting the ways in which people can make their lives better. His 1988 autobiography, *The Secret of Inner Strength— My Story,* became a bestseller.

Norris's noble work has won him new awards to go with those from his

Chuck Norris meets with U.S. Air Force Honor Guard members at Bolling Air Force Base in Washington, D.C., on June 27, 2001.

martial arts days. Among other recognitions, he won the Jewish Humanitarian Man of the Year Award, was elected to the Texas Ranger Hall of Fame, and was the army's 2001 Veteran of the Year. *Walker, Texas Ranger* won the 1998 Epiphany Award for best Christian program and its theme song, sung by Norris, won a BMI Music Television Award.

Norris and his wife, Gena O'Kelley, arrive at the first International World Stunt Awards in Santa Monica, California, on May 20, 2001.

In his later years, despite personal ordeals such as a divorce from Dianne after thirty years (Norris remarried in 1998, to Gena O'Kelley) and the challenges of being a middle-aged actor in an industry obsessed with youth, Norris continues to push himself and add to his list of accomplishments. They even extend into setting records in pastimes such as speedboat racing.

He remains close to sons Mike, an actor, and Eric, a director and stunt coordinator. He reaches out to people across the nation. He lives the life of a man who wants his example to improve the lives of others. The world is a better place because it contains Chuck Norris.

Norris's film success earned him a star on the Walk of Fame in Hollywood, California.

Filmography

Chuck Norris in Film and Television

The Wrecking Crew, 1968

Return of the Dragon, 1972

Breaker! Breaker!, 1976

Good Guys Wear Black, 1977

A Force of One, 1979

The Octagon, 1980

An Eye for an Eye, 1981

Silent Rage, 1982

Forced Vengeance, 1982

Lone Wolf McQuade, 1983

Missing in Action, 1984

Missing in Action 2: The Beginning, 1985

Code of Silence, 1985

Invasion U.S.A., 1985

Delta Force, 1986

Firewalker, 1986

Braddock: Missing in Action III, 1988

Hero and the Terror, 1988

Delta Force 2: Operation Stranglehold, 1990

The Hitman, 1991

Sidekicks, 1992

Hellbound, 1993

Top Dog, 1995

Forest Warrior, 1996

*Logan's War: Bound
by Honor,* 1998

Walker, Texas Ranger, 1993–2001
(Television show)

Chuck Norris has made many
other appearances, including starring
as himself in commercials, video
games, and talk shows. He has
appeared in several documentaries
and news reports on subjects such as
martial arts, moviemaking, and
famous friends like Bruce Lee and
Steve McQueen, as well as political
topics such as veterans, the war on
drugs, and the United Way.

Glossary

black belt The rating of "expert" in a martial art.

dojo A place where martial arts are studied.

examiner In exams for martial arts ranks, an examiner is not just the person who gives the test, but is a high master with special authority to award ranks.

grand champion In martial arts tournaments, competitors face opponents of their weight class, then the winners of each category face each other to determine the grand champion.

ippon In tournaments, the usual score is half a point. Only a particularly well done strike or kick earns a score of ippon, a full point.

M.P. Military policeman.

NCO club A lounge or bar on military bases that serves enlisted men. Officers have their own clubs.

samurai Members of the ancient Japanese warrior class. Samurai became less dominant after the late 1800s, and their fighting skills (jujitsu) were changed so to be used as a safe art form.

shodan First degree black belt, a rank that shows a student has become an expert in a Japanese or Korean martial art. Black belt ranks, or dans, can rise to as high as tenth degree, but people rarely rise higher than third.

t'ai chi chu'an A nonfighting martial art designed to promote health and calm the mind.

tang soo do Korean martial art similar to karate, using punches, kicks, and foot sweeps.

wing chun A Chinese martial art made famous by Bruce Lee, who studied it in Hong Kong.

wu shu The proper Chinese translation of "martial arts."

For More Information

Web Site

Chuck Norris's Official Web Site
http://www.chucknorris.com

Organizations

American Tang Soo Do Association
170 Pleasant Street
Malden, MA 02148
(781) 324-9568

Kick Drugs Out of America Foundation
427 West 20th Street, Suite 403
Houston, TX 77008
(713) 868-6003
Web site: http://www.kdooa.org

For Further Reading

Corcoran, John, and Emil Farkas. *Martial Arts: Traditions, History, People.* New York: Gallery Books, 1983.

Corcoran, John, and John Graden. *The Ultimate Martial Arts Q&A Book.* Chicago: Contemporary Books, 2001.

Norris, Chuck. *Chuck Norris Karate System.* Los Angeles: Fitness Media, 1973.

Norris, Chuck, and Wilmer Ames. *Toughen Up: The Chuck Norris Fitness System.* New York: Bantam, 1983.

Norris, Chuck, and Joe Hyams. *The Secret of Inner Strength: My Story.* New York: Little, Brown, & Co., 1988.

Norris, Chuck. *The Secret Power Within: Zen Solutions to Real Problems.* New York: Broadway Books, 1997.

Potts, Steve. *Learning Martial Arts.* Mankato, MN: Capstone Press, 1996.

Whitman, John. *Ghostwarrior and Other Martial Arts Stories.* Chicago: Lowell House Juvenile, 2000.

Index

109

About the Author

Dave Smeds is the author of several novels, four screenplays, and over 100 short stories, as well as nonfiction work. In addition to training in judo and aikido, for the past twenty-seven years he has intensively studied the art of goju-ryu karate under H. Donald Buck and N. Gosei Yamaguchi. A senior black belt, Dave serves on the national board of examiners of Goju-Kai Karate-Do U.S.A. and teaches goju-ryu classes in Santa Rosa, CA. For details, see his Web site at http://www.sff.net/people/DaveSmeds.

Photo Credits

Series Design and Layout

Les Kanturek